How Fruits and Vegetables Grow

Lettuce
Grows on the Ground

by Mari Schuh

Consulting Editor: Gail Saunders-Smith, PhD

Consultant: Sarah Pounders, education specialist
National Gardening Association

CAPSTONE PRESS
a capstone imprint

Pebble Books are published by Capstone Press,
1710 Roe Crest Drive, North Mankato, Minnesota 56003.
www.capstonepub.com

Books published by Capstone Press are manufactured with paper
containing at least 10 percent post-consumer waste.

Library of Congress Cataloging-in-Publication Data
Schuh, Mari C., 1975–
  Lettuce grows on the ground / by Mari Schuh.
    p. cm.—(Pebble books. How fruits and vegetables grow)
  Summary: "Simple text and photographs describe how lettuce grows on the
ground"—Provided by publisher.
  Includes bibliographical references and index.
  ISBN 978-1-4296-5281-0 (library binding)
  ISBN 978-1-4296-6188-1 (paperback)
  1. Lettuce—Juvenile literature. I. Title. II. Series: Pebble (Mankato, Minn.). How
fruits and vegetables grow.
  SB351.L6S38 2011
  635'.5—dc22   2010025472

Note to Parents and Teachers

The How Fruits and Vegetables Grow set supports national science
standards related to life science. This book describes and illustrates
how lettuce grows. The images support early readers in understanding
the text. The repetition of words and phrases helps early readers learn
new words. This book also introduces early readers to subject-specific
vocabulary words, which are defined in the Glossary section. Early
readers may need assistance to read some words and to use the Table
of Contents, Glossary, Read More, Internet Sites, and Index sections of
the book.

Printed in the United States of America in North Mankato, Minnesota.
012012
006536CGVMI

Table of Contents

On the Ground

Leafy vegetables grow
on the ground in the garden.
Their leaves grow longer
and wider in the warm sun.

Many different vegetables grow on the ground. Some have smooth leaves shaped into a ball. Others grow loose, wavy leaves.

Life Cycle of Lettuce

seeds

seedlings

lettuce

flowers

8

Growing

Lettuce is an example
of a vegetable that grows
on the ground.
Lettuce grows best
in rich, moist soil.

Lettuce seeds are planted
in cool weather.
The small seeds sprout
in about one week.

Lettuce leaves grow
from short stems.
Short roots grow
into the soil.

Lettuce grows quickly.
Leaf lettuce is often
harvested in one
or two months.

In hot weather, lettuce makes flower stalks.
The flowers make seeds.
The seeds can grow into new lettuce plants.

kale

chard

spinach

18

Other Vegetables

Many vegetables grow
on the ground like lettuce.
Kale, chard, and spinach
are other leafy vegetables
we eat.

cabbage

broccoli

cauliflower

Cabbage, broccoli, and cauliflower grow close to the ground too. Gardens are full of vegetables harvested right from the ground.

Glossary

harvest—to collect or gather crops that are ripe and ready to be eaten

moist—slightly wet

soil—earth in which plants grow

sprout—to begin to grow

stem—the main part of a plant from which leaves grow

Read More

Fine, Edith Hope, and Angela Demos Halpin. *Water, Weed, and Wait.* Berkeley, Calif.: Tricycle Press, 2010.

Pipe, Jim. *Growing Plants: Leaves, Roots, and Shoots.* Science Starters. Mankato, Minn.: Stargazer Books, 2008.

Schuh, Mari. *Growing a Garden.* Gardens. Mankato, Minn.: Capstone Press, 2010.

Internet Sites

FactHound offers a safe, fun way to find Internet sites related to this book. All of the sites on FactHound have been researched by our staff.

Here's all you do:

Visit *www.facthound.com*

Type in this code: 9781429652810

Super-cool stuff!

Check out projects, games and lots more at
www.capstonekids.com

Index

Word Count: 155
Grade: 1
Early-Intervention Level: 21

Editorial Credits
Erika L. Shores, editor; Bobbie Nuytten, designer; Wanda Winch, media researcher;
    Laura Manthe, production specialist

Photo Credits
Capstone Press: Karon Dubke, 6, 8 (top left, middle), 12, 18 (top), 20 (middle, top);
iStockphoto: Chao Yungshu, 10; Shutterstock: Denis and Yulia Pogostins, 8 (top right),
Hamiza Bakirci, 18 (middle), Juri Semjonow, Cover (roots), Larry Korb, 14, Liu Jixing,
20 (bottom), Marek Pawluczuk, 18 (bottom), Noam Armonn, 4, sunsetman, cover
(lettuce design element throughout book); www.helpinggardenersgrow.com ,
Pam Ruch, 8 (bottom), 16

The author dedicates this book to her friend Chris De Santis, who grows all sorts
of leafy green vegetables in his huge organic garden in Somers, Wisconsin.